Machines in Construction

USING SIMPLE MACHINES

Caroline Snow

PICTURE CREDITS
Cover: man hammering on house frame © Lance Nelson/Corbis/
Tranz; backhoe in Northumbria, Photodisc; chiseling a piece of rain
forest wood © Lynda Richardson/Corbis/Tranz.

page 1 © Peter Dazeley/Stone/Getty Images; page 4 (bottom left),
Corbis; page 4 (bottom right), Photodisc; page 5 (top) © Tim
Graham/Corbis/Tranz; page 5 (bottom left) © Corbis/Tranz;
page 5 (bottom right), Corbis; page 6, Photodisc; page 7 (left)
© Bettmann/Corbis/Tranz; page 7 (right) © Owen Franken/Corbis/
Tranz; page 8 © Walter Hodges/Corbis/Tranz; page 9, Corbis;
page 10 © Rosa & Rosa/Corbis/Tranz; page 11 © Richard T.
Nowitz/Corbis/Tranz; page 12 © Kathie Atkinson; page 13, Corbis;
page 14, Photodisc; page 15 © Francesco Ruggeri/Image Bank/
Getty Images; page 21, Brand X Pictures; page 29, Corbis.

Illustrations: pages 10–18 by Andrew Aguilar;
pages 23–26 by Pat Kermode.

Produced through the worldwide resources of the National
Geographic Society, John M. Fahey, Jr., President and Chief
Executive Officer; Gilbert M. Grosvenor, Chairman of the Board;
Nina D. Hoffman, Executive Vice President and President, Books
and Education Publishing Group.

PREPARED BY NATIONAL GEOGRAPHIC SCHOOL PUBLISHING
Ericka Markman, Senior Vice President and President, Children's
Books and Education Publishing Group; Steve Mico, Vice President
and Editorial Director; Marianne Hiland, Executive Editor; Richard
Easby, Editorial Manager; Jim Hiscott, Design Manager; Kristin
Hanneman, Illustrations Manager; Matt Wascavage, Manager of
Publishing Services; Sean Philpotts, Production Manager.

EDITORIAL MANAGEMENT
Morrison BookWorks, LLC

PROGRAM CONSULTANTS
Dr. Shirley V. Dickson, Program Director, Literacy, Education
Commission of the States; James A. Shymansky, E. Desmond Lee
Professor of Science Education, University of Missouri-St. Louis.

National Geographic Theme Sets program developed by Macmillan
Education Australia, Pty Limited.

Published by the National Geographic Society
1145 17th Street, N.W.
Washington, D.C. 20036-4688

ISBN: 978-0-7922-4756-2
ISBN: 0-7922-4756-6

Printed in Hong Kong.

2011 2010 2009 2008
4 5 6 7 8 9 10 11 12 13 14 15

Contents

Using Simple Machines

When you hear the word *machine*, what is the first thing that comes to your mind? Perhaps you think of a dishwasher or a vacuum cleaner. These are both machines, but a broom and a knife are also machines. Basically, a machine is any kind of device that helps you do something more easily. People use simple machines every day—at home, in sports, on construction sites, and in health care.

 ## Key Concepts ....

1. Machines use force to help people do work.
2. There are six simple machines.
3. Compound machines use two or more simple machines operating together.

Where Machines Are Found

In the Home

Simple machines help people with many different tasks in the home.

In Sports

Simple machines are a part of many types of sports equipment.

In this book you will learn about simple machines used in construction, such as this chisel.

In Construction

Simple machines make the construction of buildings possible.

In Health

Simple machines are an important part of health care.

Machines in Construction

Look at the buildings around you. Do you know how they were constructed? Think of the machines you would see on a construction site. Large earth-moving equipment and tall cranes are some of the machines you would see. You would also see workers using handheld power machines such as drills. Did you know that when construction workers use hammers and nails, they are using machines?

Simple machines are tools that make work easier for construction workers. Machines help construction workers lift, move, and cut things. Some machines have many moving parts and are made up of two or more simple machines. Many construction machines are made up of more than one simple machine.

This construction worker is using a drill. A drill is a machine often used to drive in screws.

Machines – Past and Present

Today, construction workers use machines with many parts when they build buildings. These machines help them build bigger and taller buildings. Think about very tall buildings such as the skyscrapers in a large city. Can you name some of the machines that were used to construct them?

Now think about the pyramids in Egypt. They were built thousands of years ago, by people who did not have modern tools and machines. They used only simple machines such as **wedges**, ramps, and **levers** to help them cut and move the huge stone blocks that make up the pyramids. Today, many of the machines used by construction workers are based on the same simple machines that the ancient Egyptians used.

Construction workers long ago used basic machines to help with their work.

Construction workers today also rely on machines, but most of their machines have many parts.

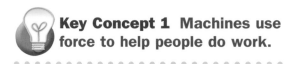

Force and Work

To understand how machines operate, you first need to understand **force** and work. Force is something that causes, changes, or stops the movement of an object. When construction workers perform a task related to building, they are always using force. They use force when they hammer nails into a surface such as wood. Force causes the hammer to hit the nail. This forces the nail to move into the wood. Construction workers use force when they lay a concrete slab. When they flatten it and smooth the top to make it level, they are using force to change its shape.

> **force**
> something that moves, changes, or stops an object

These construction workers are using force to change the surface of wet concrete.

When people such as construction workers use force to move, change, or stop something, they are doing **work**. The word *work* means many different things. Scientists define work as the result of force moving, stopping, or changing an object. Even when construction workers do an easy job, such as picking up nails, they are doing work because they cause the nails to move. On the other hand, if construction workers try very hard to lift a heavy beam, but cannot move the beam at all, they have not done work. They have used a great amount of effort, but no work has been done.

work
the result of force moving, stopping, or changing an object

People use **machines** to make work easier, or to make certain tasks possible. Machines make work easier by giving people a **mechanical advantage**. The term *mechanical advantage* refers to how much easier a machine can make a task. It can do this by changing the force needed to do work. Machines do not decrease the amount of work that needs to be done. Instead, they change the way the work is done.

machines
tools or other devices that help people do work

A hammer can be used as a machine to remove a nail from a piece of wood.

The Six Simple Machines

The six **simple machines** are basic machines that make work easier and need no fuel or electricity to power them. Simple machines change how forces act.

> **simple machines**
> devices that change how forces act

The Wedge A wedge is a simple machine that has one or more sloping sides. A wedge can end in a sharp edge, as in a chisel, or in a point, as in a nail. A smaller angle between the sides increases the mechanical advantage of a wedge. When you sharpen a chisel or knife, you reduce this angle.

People use wedges to cut, split, and pierce objects. Chisels and nails are examples of wedges used in construction. The sharp edge of a chisel allows a construction worker to chip away unwanted wood. The point and sloping sides of a nail allow it to pierce and split wood so that it can move into the wood.

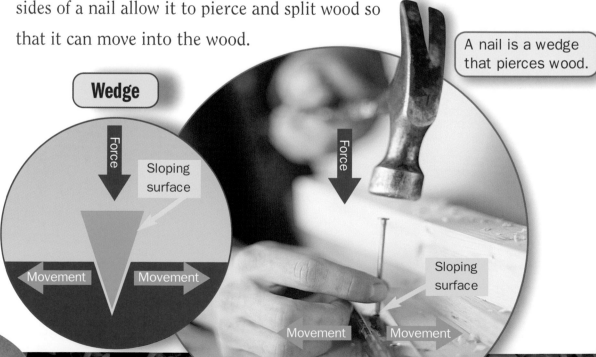

A nail is a wedge that pierces wood.

Wedge

Force

Sloping surface

Movement   Movement

Force

Sloping surface

Movement   Movement

The Lever A lever is a straight rod or bar with three parts – a load arm, a force arm, and a **fulcrum**. The load arm holds a **load**, while force is applied to the force arm. The fulcrum is the point at which the lever turns. A lever can reduce the amount of force needed to move or lift a load. A lever can also make a load move faster.

A hammer is an example of a lever. When a person uses a hammer to pull out a nail, the head of the hammer works as a fulcrum and the claw works as a load arm. The human arm is also a useful lever. When a person hammers in a nail, his or her elbow becomes a fulcrum. The arm muscles supply force that moves the hammer.

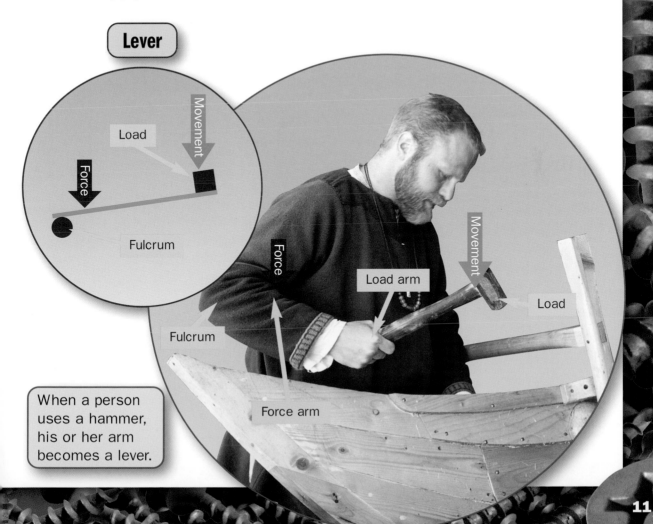

Lever

Load

Movement

Force

Fulcrum

Force

Load arm

Movement

Load

Fulcrum

Force arm

When a person uses a hammer, his or her arm becomes a lever.

The Inclined Plane An **inclined plane**, or ramp, is a flat, slanted surface with a low end and a high end. Inclined planes make it easier to move objects up. Instead of lifting an object straight up, you can push or pull the object up the inclined plane. For example, pushing a wheelbarrow up a ramp is easier than lifting it up the same distance.

Ramps or inclined planes make work easier by reducing the amount of force needed to move an object up. The less steep the inclined plane is, the easier the job becomes. An inclined plane allows you to use a smaller force over a greater distance to lift an object.

Inclined Plane

High end

Load

Force

Low end

Slanted surface

Load

Force

Low end

Slanted surface

High end

This inclined plane helps construction workers move objects up.

The Screw   A **screw** is an inclined plane that is twisted into a spiral around a pole. This twisted ramp is called the screw's **thread**. When a screw is turned, the thread twists into the object that is at the tip of the screw. Think of two screws of the same length, but one with more thread than the other. Imagine inserting them both to the same depth in a piece of wood. It would take more turns but less force to insert the screw with more thread. This is because the thread would not be as steep as on the screw with less thread. As with any inclined plane, decreasing the steepness of the slope reduces the force needed to do work.

A screw must be turned as it is inserted. It can be removed by turning it in the opposite direction.

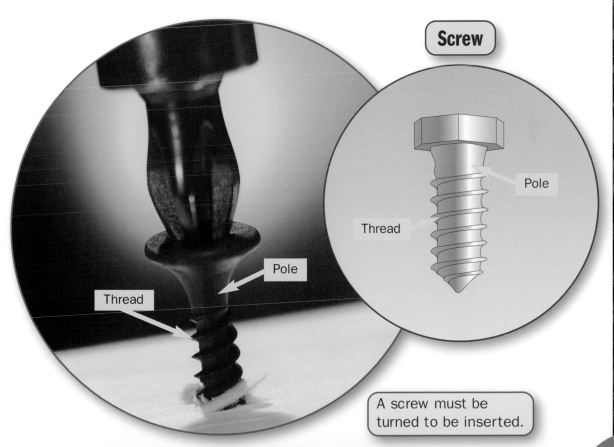

Screw

Pole

Thread

Pole

Thread

A screw must be turned to be inserted.

The Wheel and Axle A **wheel and axle** is an important simple machine. It can change the force required to turn an object. This machine has a wheel that turns on a pole called an axle. A wheel and axle are attached so that they turn together. Turning the larger wheel a long distance turns the smaller axle a shorter distance, but with stronger force. Or, a strong force applied to the axle can be used to turn the wheel a greater distance.

A screwdriver is a wheel and axle. The thick handle is the wheel and the metal shaft is the axle. When a construction worker turns the handle of the screwdriver, the handle turns a long way. The smaller shaft turns a shorter distance, but with more force. This change in force makes it easier for the worker to drive a screw into a piece of wood.

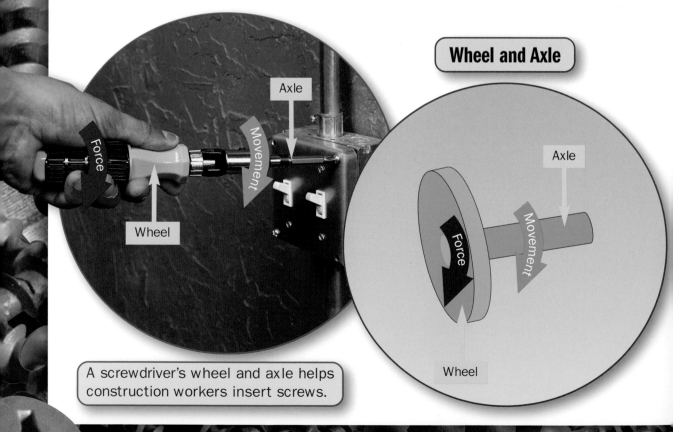

Wheel and Axle

Axle

Movement

Force

Wheel

Axle

Force

Movement

Wheel

A screwdriver's wheel and axle helps construction workers insert screws.

The Pulley A **pulley** also has a wheel and an axle. But the pulley has a grooved wheel that spins on an axle that does not turn. A rope in the groove hangs down on both sides of the wheel. One end of the rope is attached to a load. By pulling on the other end of the rope, a person can lift the load. With a basic pulley, the amount of force needed to lift the load is equal to the weight of the load. The pulley makes the work easier by changing the direction of the force, because pulling down can be easier than lifting up.

Some machines have more than one pulley. When two or more pulleys are used together, they can lessen the amount of force needed to lift a load. Pulleys are useful on construction sites as a way of lifting heavy loads to high places.

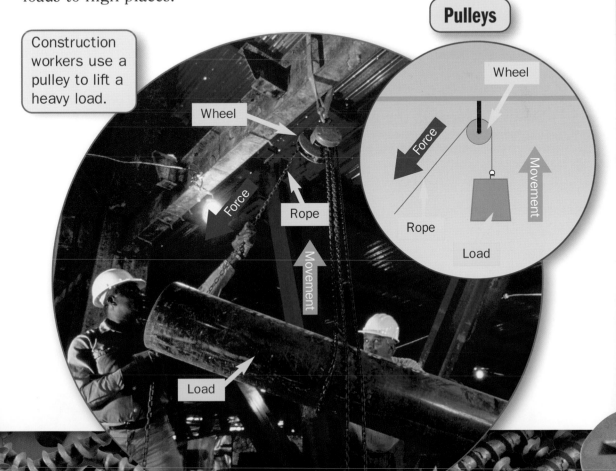

Construction workers use a pulley to lift a heavy load.

Pulleys

Wheel

Force

Rope

Movement

Load

Wheel

Force

Rope

Movement

Load

Key Concept 3 Compound machines use two
or more simple machines operating together.

Working with Machines in Construction

Building is hard work that requires a great amount of force, so
construction workers use machines to make their work easier.

Some machines used in construction are made
up of just one simple machine. Some are a
combination of two or more simple machines.
Machines that are made up of more than one
simple machine are called **compound machines**.

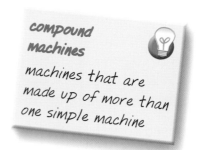

compound
machines

machines that are
made up of more than
one simple machine

Shovel A shovel is an example of a lever
and a wedge. The blade of a shovel is a
wedge. When the shovel is used to push up
earth, it acts as a lever. The fixed point at
which the blade turns in the ground is the
fulcrum. The sharper the blade and the
longer the handle, the greater the
mechanical advantage.

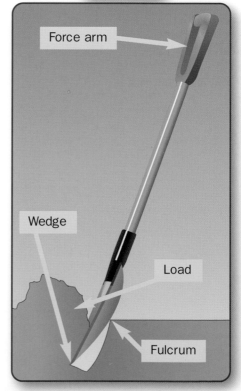

Shovel

Force arm

Wedge

Load

Fulcrum

Cement Mixer A cement mixer is a compound machine. This machine mixes sand, water, and a special powder to make cement. A cement mixer has a motor that turns a pulley. The movement of the pulley turns the drum, mixing its contents. A cement mixer also uses another simple machine—the lever. A lever holds the drum in place until the cement mix is ready to be poured out. When you pull the lever, the drum is released. Then the mixer's handwheel can be used to tip the drum for emptying. The handwheel is a wheel and axle.

Cement Mixer

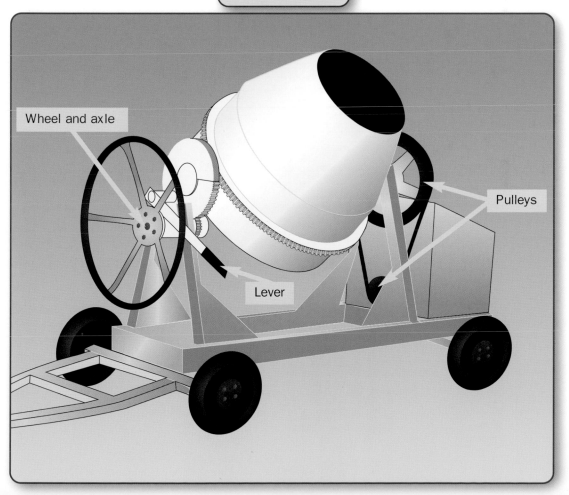

Wheel and axle

Pulleys

Lever

Crane A crane is a big machine that is used at construction sites. It uses pulleys to lift and move heavy loads. A crane picks up a load using a strong steel cable that loops around a series of pulleys. The strong cable can hold very heavy loads. One end of the cable winds around a winch, or a rotating drum. The crane's motor connects to the winch and turns it around to wind the cable in or let it out. The cable is wound in to lift loads and wound out to lower them. Cranes usually have more than one pulley wheel. Using more than one pulley reduces the force needed to lift a load, giving the crane a mechanical advantage.

Crane

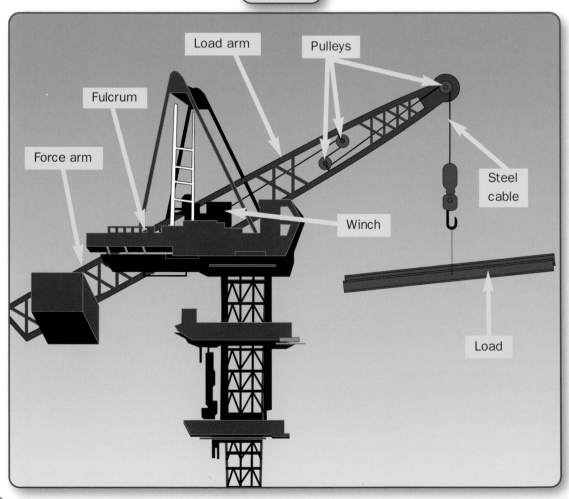

Load arm

Pulleys

Fulcrum

Force arm

Steel cable

Winch

Load

Think About the **Key Concepts**

Think about what you read. Think about the pictures and diagrams. Use these to answer the questions. Share what you think with others.

1. What are three things that force can do to an object? Give an example of each.

2. In science, what is the connection between force and work?

3. Name the six simple machines. Explain how each one can help people work.

4. Give two examples of compound machines. Explain how they help people work.

Labeled Photograph

Photographs show you real-life examples of ideas discussed in books or articles.

A **labeled photograph** provides extra information. The labels show you which important parts of the photograph you should be looking at.

Look back at the labeled photographs on pages 10–15. These are labeled examples of simple machines used in construction. The labeled photograph on page 21 is an example of a compound machine used in construction: a vise.

How to Read a Labeled Photograph

1. **Read the title.**

   The title tells you the subject, or what the photograph is about.

2. **Read the labels and caption.**

   Labels and captions tell you about the subject and its parts.

3. **Study the photograph.**

   Connect the information in the photograph to what you have read in the text.

Vise

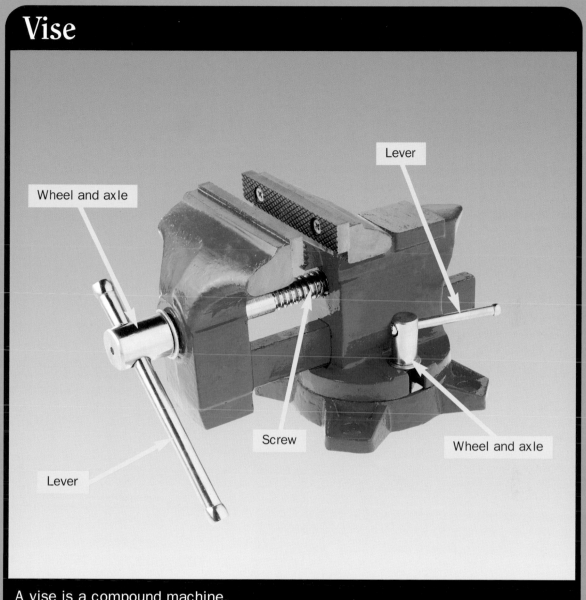

Lever

Wheel and axle

Lever

Screw

Wheel and axle

A vise is a compound machine.

What Can You See?

Read the photograph by following the steps on page 20. Now look back at the diagrams of compound machines on pages 16–18. Can you draw a basic diagram showing the simple machines in a vise?

How-to Books

The purpose of **how-to books** is to give directions. How-to books take many forms.

You use different how-to books to find out how to do different things. If you want to know how to use a machine, you read a **user manual**. User manuals come with machines when you buy them.

User manuals give you all the information you need to know before you use a machine. They tell you how to operate the machine. They also tell you how to care for the machine and how to use it safely.

Power Drill User Manual

Congratulations on buying your new power drill. Inside this user manual, you will find directions on using your power drill. You will also learn how to clean and care for it. Follow these instructions, and you will get many years of use from your power drill.

The **title** tells you which machine the user manual is for.

Parts of the Power Drill

Subheads break the information into easy-to-find sections.

Labels show the parts of the machine.

1. chuck jaws
2. chuck
3. gear selector
4. forward or reverse switch
5. trigger switch
6. handle
7. power cord
8. power plug
9. drill bits

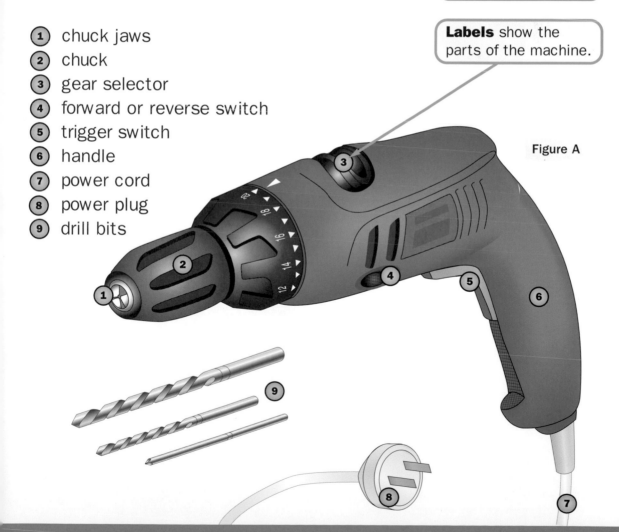

Figure A

Safety Precautions

Great care needs to be taken when you use a power drill. It is important to follow these safety instructions.

- Always wear safety glasses to protect your eyes (Figure B). Parts of the material you are drilling into can fly back at you.

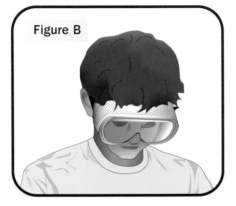

Figure B

- Do not use the power drill near water or when it is raining. This may result in electric shock.

- Do not drill where there may be electrical wires. This may also result in electric shock.

- Do not try to fix the power drill yourself if it stops working. Always take it to a service center.

- Always unplug the power drill from the power supply when you are not using it.

Important information is presented in bulleted lists so it is easy to find and read.

Setting Up the Power Drill

Fitting the Drill Bit

Different sizes and types of drill bits are designed to make holes in different materials. Use the drill bit best suited for the job. Follow these steps to fit the bit into the drill.

- Make sure that the forward or reverse switch is locked.

- Hold the rear part of the chuck. Rotate the front part of the chuck until the jaws open (Figure C).

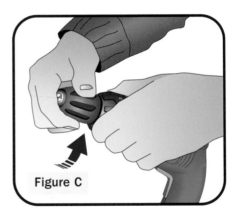

Figure C

- Place the drill bit in the chuck jaws.

- Hold the rear part of the chuck. Rotate the front part of the chuck until the jaws have a firm grip on the drill bit.

Using the Power Drill

Drilling a Hole

- Before drilling a hole, mark with a pencil where you want to place the hole.

- Put the switch into the forward position.

- Line the power drill up with the pencil mark. The drill should be at right angles to the surface you are drilling.

- Gently push your finger on the trigger switch (Figure D). The drill bit will go into the material.

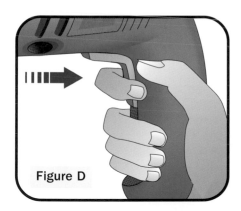

Figure D

Drilling with Care

Take care not to damage the drill.

- Do not push too hard on the drill when you are using it. This could damage the motor.

- Always use sharp drill bits.

Inserting a Screw

You can use the power drill to insert a screw in a wall.

- Select a screwdriver bit.

- Mark with a pencil where you want to place the screw.

- Put the switch into the forward position (Figure E).

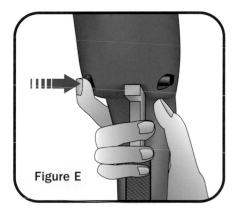

Figure E

- Hold the screw firmly up to the pencil mark. The screw should be at right angles to the wall.

- Fit the bit into the screw.

- Push on the trigger switch. The screw will go into the wall.

Removing a Screw

You can also use the power drill to remove screws.

- Select a screwdriver bit.

- Put the switch into the reverse position.

- Fit the bit into the screw.

- Push on the trigger switch.

Caring for the Power Drill

Cleaning the Chuck

Clean the chuck after every use to keep the power drill working smoothly.

- Unplug the power drill.
- Rotate the chuck to open the jaws to their widest point. Remove the drill bit (Figure F).

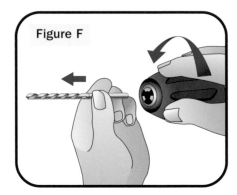

Figure F

- Tap out the sawdust from inside the chuck.
- Vacuum or brush the chuck to remove any extra dust.

Caring for the Parts

After much use, power drill parts such as drill bits can become worn and will not work well.

- Check the parts of the power drill regularly.
- Take any parts that are worn or damaged to a service center where the parts can be replaced.

Storing the Power Drill

It is important to store the power drill carefully to keep it in good working order.

- Keep the drill and its parts in the case provided when you are not using it (Figure G).

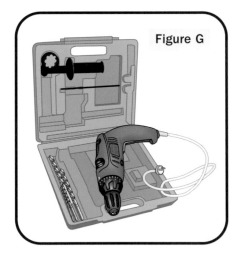

Figure G

- Store the drill in a clean, dry place, away from water pipes or sinks.
- Never leave the drill outside when you are not using it.

Apply the **Key Concepts**

Key Concept 1 Machines use force to help people do work.

Activity

Think of four ways that people do work in construction. Create a concept web to show the different types of work. For each type of work, write whether the force moves, stops, or changes an object. Label the center of your concept web "Work and Construction."

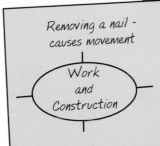

Removing a nail - causes movement

Work and Construction

Key Concept 2 There are six simple machines.

Activity

Think of two examples of simple machines found in construction. Draw these machines. Then label the parts that make them simple machines.

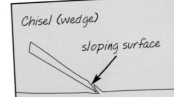

Chisel (wedge)

sloping surface

Key Concept 3 Compound machines use two or more simple machines operating together.

Activity

Draw two compound machines found in construction. Then label the different simple machines found within them. One has been started for you on the right.

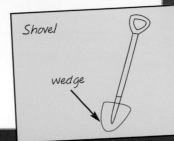

Shovel

wedge

Write
Your Own
User Manual

You have read the user manual for the power drill. Now you can think of a different machine that is used in construction and write a user manual for it.

1. Study the Model

Look back at the user manual on pages 23–26. What information is presented under each section? How do bulleted lists make the information easy to find and read? How do diagrams help you understand the information in the user manual?

2. Choose a Machine

Think of a machine that is used in construction. Draw the design of your machine. Make notes on what job the machine does and how the machine operates. Think of any safety precautions users will need to be told about.

User Manual

◆ Present the information in bulleted lists.

◆ Use diagrams to support the text.

◆ Break the information into easy-to-find sections.

◆ Include important safety precautions.

3. Write a User Manual

Use subheads that are similar to the ones in the power drill user manual to write a user manual for your machine. Present the important information clearly in bulleted lists.

Safety Precautions

- Wear safety glasses when using the machine.

- Unplug the machine after use.

- Keep the machine out of reach of children.

4. Draw Diagrams

Draw a diagram and label the different parts of your machine. Label all the parts that you refer to in the text. Then draw smaller diagrams to help illustrate the information in your bulleted lists.

5. Read over Your Work

Read over your user manual, correcting any spelling mistakes or punctuation errors. Make sure your user manual is easy to understand. Are your instructions for use easy to follow? Have you listed all the safety precautions? Did you describe how to care for the machine? Do your diagrams clearly illustrate the text? Is there any other information the user of your machine might need to know?

Present Your Machine

Now that you have chosen a machine and written a user manual for it, you can present the machine to the rest of the class.

How to Present Your Machine

1. Copy your labeled diagram onto an overhead transparency.

Draw the diagram clearly so you can show the different parts of your machine to the class.

2. Explain your machine to the class.

Take turns presenting your machines. Show the class the different parts of your machine on the overhead projector. Explain to the class what the machine is used for and how the machine works.

3. Explain the safety precautions.

It is important to follow the safety precautions carefully when you use any machine. Tell the class of any possible dangers with using your machine. Explain how to use the machine in the safest way possible.

4. Show the class how to care for the machine.

Tell the class how to clean, store, and care for the parts of your machine to keep it in the best working order.

Glossary

compound machines – machines that are made up of more than one simple machine

force – something that moves, changes, or stops an object

fulcrum – the fixed point on which a lever turns or swivels

inclined plane – a slanted surface that is higher at one end than the other; also called a ramp

levers – straight bars or rods that rotate about a fixed place

load – an object that a simple machine moves, stops, or changes

machines – tools or other devices that help people do work

mechanical advantage – the extent to which a machine changes force and direction

pulley – a grooved wheel and rope system, used to move loads

screw – a pole with a ridge called a thread that spirals around it

simple machines – devices that change how forces act

thread – a sloped ridge that wraps around the pole of a screw

wedges – objects with one or more sloping sides that may end in a sharp edge or point

wheel and axle – a wheel joined to a pole or rod

work – the result of force moving, stopping, or changing an object

Index